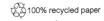

The
Red and White
Spotted
Handkerchief

*"This little hanky
on my back
sets me travelling
down the track.*

*"I'm a traveller now,"
says Jack.*

Have you read Tony Mitton's first
fantastic poetry book ?

Plum

Don't be so glum,
plum.

Don't feel beaten.

You were made
to be eaten.

But don't you know
that deep within,
beneath your juicy flesh
and flimsy skin,

you bear a mystery,
you hold a key,

you have the making of
a whole new tree.

The
Red and White Spotted Handkerchief

Tony Mitton

Illustrated by
Peter Bailey

■SCHOLASTIC

Scholastic Children's Books,
Commonwealth House, 1–19 New Oxford Street
London WC1A 1NU, UK
a division of Scholastic Ltd
London ~ New York ~ Toronto ~ Sydney ~ Auckland
Mexico City ~ New Delhi ~ Hong Kong

First published by Scholastic Ltd, 2000
This edition, 2001

Text copyright © Tony Mitton, 2000
Illustrations copyright © Peter Bailey, 2000

ISBN 0 439 99407 1

Typeset by Rowland Phototypesetting Ltd, Bury St Edmunds, Suffolk
Printed by Cox & Wyman Ltd, Reading, Berks

10 9 8 7 6 5 4 3 2 1

Contents

To Elizabeth
This little story, deep and true,
I dedicate, my love, to you.
If you'll be Jill, then I'll be Jack.
Together we can take the track
and find our way, through good and ill,
to happiness on Dragon Hill.

The
Red and White
Spotted
Handkerchief

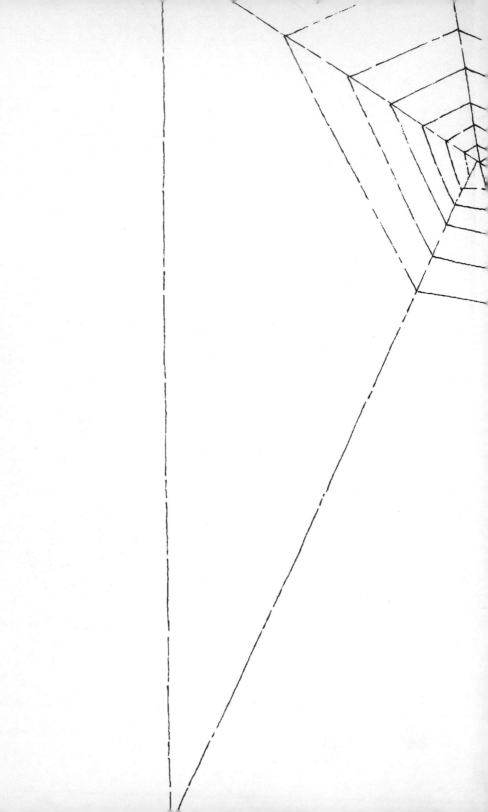

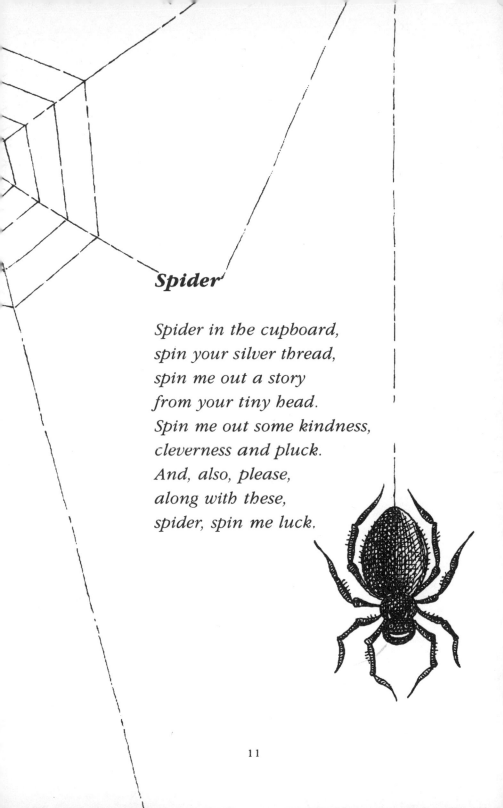

Spider

Spider in the cupboard,
spin your silver thread,
spin me out a story
from your tiny head.
Spin me out some kindness,
cleverness and pluck.
And, also, please,
along with these,
spider, spin me luck.

When Jack looked into his cupboard
to get some supper there,
all he found was a loaf of bread,
a cobweb and empty air.

So, early the very next morning,
up got our boy Jack.
He wrapped the crusts from the night before
in a spotted hanky pack.

"I may be poor," he said to himself,
"but I'm also bright and bold.
So I'm off to seek adventure
and, who knows, maybe gold?"

Hanky

"This little hanky,
red and white,
will make a pack
that's small and light.

"This little hanky,
white and red,
will wrap my hopes up
with my bread.

"This little hanky
on my back
sets me travelling
down the track.

"I'm a traveller now,"
says Jack.

Now, as Jack went a-walking,
he came upon a stone,
and sitting there in silence
was an old and ragged crone.

"My way is long and hungry,"
she croaked to Master Jack.
So Jack undid his hanky
and shared his simple snack.

Bread

Bread from yeast
and ears of wheat,

Bread that's dark
and rich to eat,

Bread that grows
from Mother Earth,

Hunger knows
what bread is worth.

"Your heart is full of kindness,"
the old crone croaked to Jack.
"So, in return, I'll show to you
a strange and secret track."

"This is an old forgotten way
that winds down to the sea.
Follow its trail and do not fail
to keep this lucky key."

Key

An ancient key,
a curious key,
kept in an old crone's frock.
And shall we see
what such a key
can open or unlock?

Is it the key to a dungeon?
Is it the key to a door?
Or is it the key
to the mystery
of a hidden treasure store?

Is it the key to a fetter,
to a chain, or a gold-filled crock?
Shall we ever see
what such a key
may luckily unlock?

So Jack set off and soon he came
to the edge of the open sea.
And there on the rocks was a mermaid
who wept most bitterly.

"Please tell," said Jack in kindness,
"what causes you such wrong?"
She gave a sigh with her sad reply,
"Oh sir, I've lost my song."

Mermaid

Marvellous maiden
from under the sea,
you glimmer with magic
and mystery.
Your scales are green silver.
Your hair glints with gold.
And your song is a wonder
that cannot be told.

Marvellous maiden,
you'll lull me to sleep.
Then you'll carry me down
to your cave in the deep.
I must stay above,
no, I cannot come down,
for if I go with you
I surely shall drown.

"A sea-song's often found," said Jack,
"wherever the tide laps near."
He stooped and picked a seashell up
and held it to her ear.

"Oh, clever Jack," the mermaid cried.
"A song of wind and sea!
Now here's an ocean curio,
a gift for helping me."

Seashell

Walk beside the waters
with the falling tide.
Find a shell.
Try to tell
the song you hear inside.

Strange and winding sea-maze,
say, how can it be
the secret space,
the hidden place,
will sing of wind and sea?

Jack took the gift. It seemed to be
an Oriental flask.
But as he pulled the stopper
he had no need to ask.

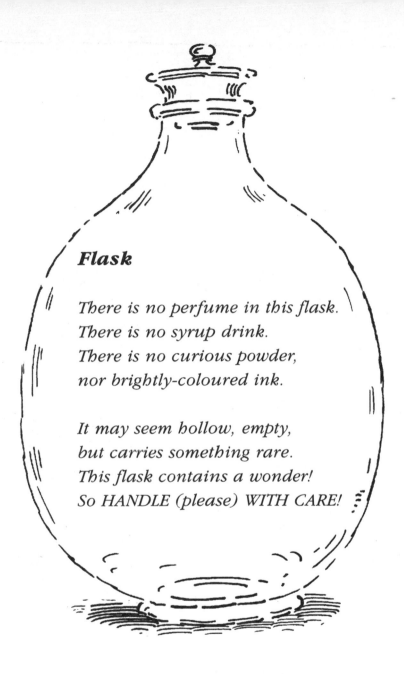

Flask

There is no perfume in this flask.
There is no syrup drink.
There is no curious powder,
nor brightly-coloured ink.

It may seem hollow, empty,
but carries something rare.
This flask contains a wonder!
So HANDLE (please) WITH CARE!

A genie billowed out and begged,
"Oh, Master, set me free.
I feel that I've been bottled up
for all eternity!"

"A life inside a flask!" cried Jack.
"Why, that's no way to live!
I wish you back your freedom,
if freedom's mine to give."

"Young Jack is kind," the genie grinned,
making a grateful bow.
"Accept this magic carpet.
I shall not need it now."

Carpet

Colourful carpet,
your curious patterns
are woven with whispers of sky.
No wonder you float
like a beautiful boat
whenever you hover and fly.

Colourful carpet,
the silk of your tassels
is twisted from twitters of bird.
No wonder you fly
to the end of the sky
whenever I give you the word.

Jack climbed onto the carpet
and chanted, "Carpet, fly!
Away to a magic island,
to a place where sea meets sky."

And there he met with a castaway
who longed for his old home shore,
and asked him to trade the carpet
for a map to a treasure store.

Island

Island of secrets
and whispery trees.
Island of bird-calls
that riddle the breeze.
Island of forests
and silvery sands
where fairies go singing
in sinister bands.
Island of caverns
that burrow down deep
where treasure and danger
lie hidden asleep.

Island of mystery
locked in a spell.
What is your secret?
Oh, open and tell!

Map

Whoever finds this ancient scrap
of parchment, see – it is a map.
It may be tattered, torn and old,
but oh! – it holds the key to gold.
Follow the path, trace the trail
and do not let your courage fail.
Enter the cavern, boldly tread
the rumbling burrow, the winding thread.
Trust your honest heart, good friend,
to find the treasure at the end.

"A treasure map!" young Jack cried out.
"Why, that's the thing for me!
Yes, take the rug, my ragged friend.
Fly home across the sea."

Then Jack knelt down upon the sand
to see what he had got.
And on his map a cave was shown,
and a red X marked the spot.

Jack went roaming the island
till he came in sight of the cave.
But a fairy band came and took his hand,
crying, "See, this lad looks brave!"

"Go down, brave boy, and get the gold
or we'll beat you black and blue.
But, boy, beware the dragon,
for the dragon might get you!"

Fairies

We are the sinister fairies.
We're vicious and greedy and bad.
We wait by the cave for a traveller brave,
a lively young lass or a lad.

We are all hungry for treasure,
but we dare not go under the ground.
For we fear a death from the fiery breath
and we don't like the rumbly sound.

We are all jealous for jewellery,
green emeralds, rubies of red.
But we will not go down, no, not for a crown...
We'd rather send YOU instead!

So Jack went down through the darkness
till he came to the end of the track.
"Is there anyone there?" he softly called.
"Just me!" a voice growled back.

"I'm a sad and lonely dragon,
locked up with a magic chain.
And the wizard who took the magic key
has never been seen again."

Dragon

Under the earth
where treasure lies deep
there are fearsome dragons
half-asleep.

You may hear them snuffle,
wheeze and sigh,
or catch a glimpse
of a watchful eye.

And if you're a touch
too greedy or bold,
a shade too eager
to grab the gold,

you won't get rich
on jewels and cash.
You'll end up scorched
to smouldering ash!

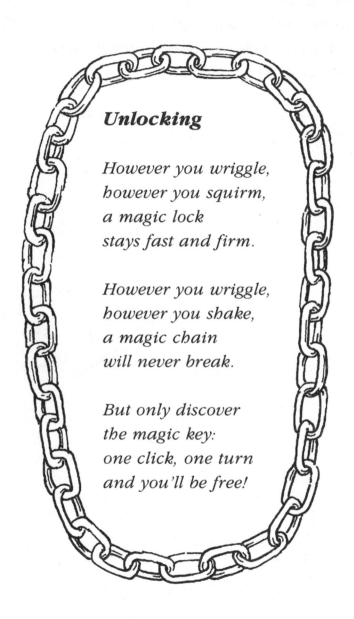

Unlocking

However you wriggle,
however you squirm,
a magic lock
stays fast and firm.

However you wriggle,
however you shake,
a magic chain
will never break.

But only discover
the magic key:
one click, one turn
and you'll be free!

"I have a lucky key..." said Jack.
"Who knows? It just might fit..."
He tried the lock. It clicked and turned.
The dragon cried, "That's it!"

"I'm free at last, you clever lad.
So help yourself to treasure.
Then mount my back. We'll fly away
and live a life of leisure."

"But up above the fairies wait…"
young Jack began to say.
"Fairies? Pah!" the dragon scoffed.
"I'll see them on their way."

So, with Jack firmly mounted,
along the cave they sped.
And, as they blasted from its mouth,
the frightened fairies fled.

Dragonpower

Do you know what the power
of a dragon is worth?
It is drawn from the fire
at the heart of the earth,
from the pull of the moon,
from the push of the sun,
from the lightning forks
as they crackle and run,
from the sweep of the wind,
from the sway of the sea,
from all of the natural
powers that be.

When a dragon is speeding
(I hardly need say)
nothing dare stop it
or stand in its way.

The dragon crossed the ocean,
our boy upon its back.
And soon the two flew into view
of Jack's old crumbling shack.

And there, before Jack's little home,
beside the small, green hill,
the dragon turned into a girl.
"Hello," she said. "I'm Jill."

Spell

Have you heard the stories tell
how strange enchantment, binding spell,
can take a body, change its shape
and turn a man into an ape,
a boy into a barking dog,
a handsome prince into a frog?
Is it then so very strange,
a spell, that has such power to change,
should give a stretch, a twist, a curl
and make a dragon from a girl?
And surely we'd expect that Jack
should find the way to change her back?

Jack's journey's done. His story's told.
And Jack and Jill have used their gold.
They've been to market, set up farm,
and here we see them, arm in arm.

Jill has Jack, and Jack has Jill.
And here they live on Dragon Hill.

And yes, it's me,
Jack's spider friend,
to weave those magic words:
The End

The
Strayaway
Child

For Doris, from Papa

The strayaway child stepped out from her
    cottage,
out from a world full of tears and of dust,
out from a world full of crust and of porridge,
leaving behind all the *don't* and the *must*.

Voice

Leave behind your dolly.
Leave behind your bear.
Leave behind your open book
lying on the chair.

Leave behind the boredom
that lingers round your bed.
Listen to the little voice
that whispers in your head.

The strayaway child stepped into the forest,
into the maze of the whispering wood.
She slipped through the gate at the end of the
    garden.
She wouldn't stay home and she wouldn't be
    good.

She passed from the daylight and into the
  shadows,
over the borders of dream and of fear.
She parted the branches and entered the
  greenwood.
She peered through the darkness and pricked
  up her ear.

Welcome

Come near, child. Come near.
Forget fancies, forget fear.
Leave behind ought and should.
Let go of bad and good.
Welcome to branch and root.
Welcome to leaf and fruit.
Welcome, welcome,
welcome to the wood.

The strayaway child looked up at the
  branches.
Was it a flutter or rustle she heard?
And there in a dapple of leafshade and
  sunlight
she made out the shape of a bright yellow
  bird.

It cocked its small head and it ruffled its
  feathers.
It flew to her hand with a flitter of wing.
It flapped and it fussed as it pecked at her
  fingers.
It opened its beak and it started to sing.

Bird

Do you like a flutter?
Do you like fun?
I'm a ball of feather,
bright as the sun.

Listen to the song
my small bill sings.
I'll light you through the forest
like a lantern on wings!

The little bird flew and the strayaway followed
along a tight track where it led through the
   trees.
And there in a clearing they met with a
   woodman
whose bundle had brought the old man to his
   knees.

"You are old," said the girl, "and your burden
 is heavy.
Now where are you going to, may I enquire?"
"I am bound," said the man, "for the heart of
 the forest.
A little old lady's in need of a fire."

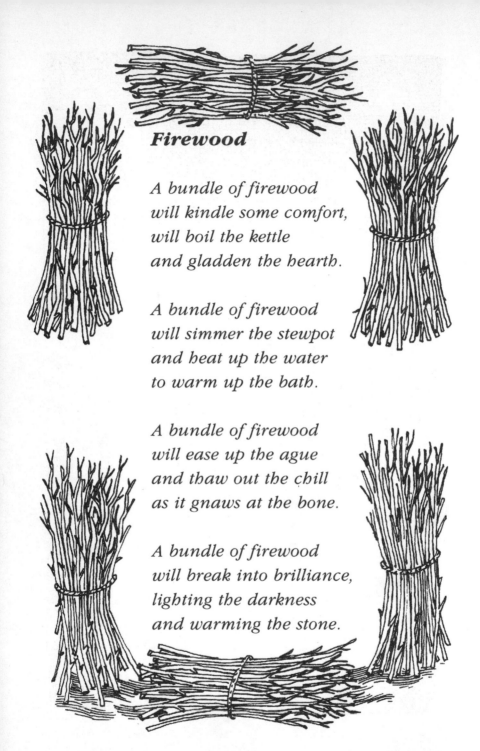

Firewood

A bundle of firewood
will kindle some comfort,
will boil the kettle
and gladden the hearth.

A bundle of firewood
will simmer the stewpot
and heat up the water
to warm up the bath.

A bundle of firewood
will ease up the ague
and thaw out the chill
as it gnaws at the bone.

A bundle of firewood
will break into brilliance,
lighting the darkness
and warming the stone.

Fire

Deep in the heart
of wood I lie sleeping.
But draw me out, wake me,
and I will come leaping.
I'll dance in the darkness
with limbs full of light,
and I'll warm up the world
with my dangerous delight.

The strayaway picked up the bundle and
   carried it,
taking the trackway that led through the
   wood,
till they came to a cottage tucked snug in a
   clearing,
and there in the doorway an old woman
   stood.

She carried the firewood over the threshold.
The heart of that cottage was chilly and cold.
But, as the fire kindled and flames began
    crackling,
the cottage grew cheerful with warmth and
    with gold.

The old woman sat and she told them a story,
passing her fingers in front of the fire.
The strayaway watched as those withered old
    fingers
span from the brightness a flickering wire.

"Far through the forest," she said, "grows a
    garden.
And there in the garden an apple tree stands.
The apples are magic, but if you would pluck
    one,
take this bright wire I weave in my hands."

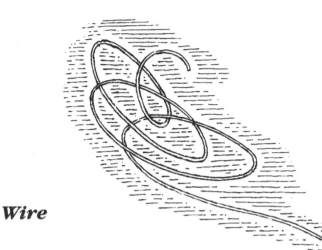

Wire

Glistening, glimmering, glinting wire,
spun from playful, flickering fire,
What will you tie or tightly bind?
What will you weave? Where will you wind?

Golden strand, oh glistering string,
what strange fortune might you bring?

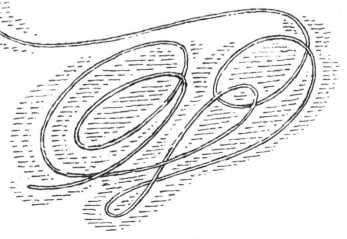

The strayaway set off to search for the
    garden.
The old woman told her to follow a stream.
The journey was long. She grew footsore and
    weary,
until that it seemed she was treading a dream.

The little bird flew through the branches
    above her.
It shone like a flickering light overhead.
It led her to nut trees and clustering berries,
and found her sweet bracken to make her a
    bed.

Stream

Follow the stream where it sparkles.
Start where it bubbles and springs.
Go where it dashes and dances.
Hear how it babbles and sings.

Follow its course through the forest,
as it gambols along in its glee.
Go where it flashes and prances
till it takes you to where you
    would be.

But one day they came to a wall and a
  gateway.
The gates they were fastened and peeling
  with rust.
And under a tree slept an old, bearded
  minstrel.
His lute lay unstrung by his side in the dust.

He woke as they came, and he started to
    stammer,
"The gates open only when I start to play.
But it's years since I've sung, and my song is
    forgotten.
My lute has lain silent for many a day."

Neglect

Day nor night,
early nor late,
nobody calls
at the old, locked gate.

Day nor night,
late nor soon,
neither by sunlight
nor by moon.

Neither by moonshine,
nor sun-dapple,
nobody seeks
the magic apple.

Nobody seeks it,
nobody finds.
Nobody cares
and nobody minds.

The strayaway reached out her hand to the
   minstrel
and showed him the coil of the old woman's
   wire.
It lay in her palm like a handful of sunlight,
a-tingle with music and brimming with fire.

The old minstrel took up his lute and he
   strung it.
He threaded the strings and he twisted them
   tight.
Then his old fingers started to pluck out a
   melody,
filling the forest with charm and delight.

Song

Song like liquid, like fire.
Words full of joy and desire.
Melody twisting and flowing.
Mind knowing
glimpses of magical power.

Song you can tell, but not touch,
swelling so much.
Song you can hear, but not hold,
ghost of pure gold.
Song you can feel, but not see,
creating a key
to open and enter the heart,
breaking the locked gates apart.

The gates of the garden swung silently open.
The breeze seemed to shimmer, the leaves
    seemed to dance.
The bird led the girl till she stood at the
    centre
and gazed at the tree in a magical trance.

The tree was a-quiver with sunlight and
  birdsong.
Its fruit seemed to glisten with promise and
  charm.
She stretched out to pluck one and, as she
  reached upward,
it fell from the branch and it dropped to her
  palm.

Apple

What can you do
with an apple of happiness?
Bite it and swallow it
down to the core?

Or stash it in secret
away in a cupboard,
hide it and hoard it
and hope to get more?

Plant all the pips
in your garden or orchard,
hope to grow tree-loads
to crop and to sell?

Or hold it quite humbly
and carry it with you,
and wait for the moment
to ripen and tell?

Suddenly, out of the depths of the bushes,
a furious guardian burst with a roar.
It came for the girl with a snarl and a
    grimace,
slashing its talons and gnashing its jaw.

Monster

Never far from happiness,
just at the edge of joy,
a monster waits in hiding
to devour or destroy.

Always close to pleasure,
crouched beside content,
it watches for its moment
to batter, bruise or dent.

Seek the apple of happiness.
Hold it if you dare.
But mind out for the monster.
He's hungry, so BEWARE!

Quick as a cinder that flies from the fire
the little bird pointed a path with its beak.
The strayaway followed, her heart full of
    panic.
No time to hesitate. No time to speak.

Out of the garden the bird and the girl flew,
into the heat of the day and the dust.
And there by the wayside they met a young
    beggarmaid,
pleading with them for a coin or a crust.

The girl gave the poor-child the wonderful
    apple.
It glowed as she bit it. Her hunger fell still.
But the little bird fussed at the core in the
    roadway.
She pecked out a pip to keep tucked in her
    bill.

Want

Down any road or way or lane,
down any path or track,
you'll meet with need or misery,
with hunger, pain or lack.

You'll meet with many kinds of want
wherever people live.
So will you shrug and turn away?
Or will you stay and give?

They went down the road till they came to a
   dwelling.
The garden lay wasted, the cottage was bare.
The windows were cobwebbed, the hearth
   cold and empty.
Only the beetle and spider lived there.

The strayaway looked, and it filled her with
   sadness.
She thought of a cottage she'd left far behind.
She thought of her mother, her father, her
   brother,
remembering a home that was cosy and kind.

Home

If you should go wandering into the forest,
on down the valley or over the hill,
you'll come to a point, whether later or early,
when eagerness falters and spirits fall still.

Whatever adventure, whatever excitement,
you meet on your way as you recklessly roam,
you'll come to a place where you pause for a
     moment
and all of your longings turn only to home.

The little bird beckoned her on down the
    trackway.
They came to a hill-path she thought that she
    knew.
And when she had climbed it, she looked
    down below her.
She let out a gasp as she took in the view.

There was her cottage, so close by the forest.
A ribbon of smoke drifted up from its stack.
The strayaway ran and the little bird fluttered.
Soon they were there by the gate at the back.

Circle

How strange to think a journey
down some mysterious lane
will lead you through adventures
and bring you back again.

How strange to think that travelling
down fortune's dusty track
will bring you rich experience
and bring you wisely back.

How strange to play with tricky chance
and give its wheel a spin,
and go where it will take you
to be back where you begin.

The little bird fluttered and fussed in the
  orchard.
She planted the pip and she sang it a song.
The strayaway stood in the gateway and
  faltered.
Had she been foolish? Had she done wrong?

There, as she troubled, unsure in the orchard,
under the dapple of gold and of green,
her parents came anxiously running toward
  her,
"Oh where, little wanderer, where have you
  been?"

Return

Perhaps I look muddled
and muddied and mazed.

And maybe I'm wildered
and weary and crazed.

But I'm back from the forest,
I'm fine and I'm well.

And here in my head
I've a story to tell.

The strayaway child grew up in her cottage,
there on the edge of the whispering wood,
there in a garden of apples and sunlight,
a home that was happy and growing and
good.

Pip

"Pip, pip," says yellow bird,
"Rain come and water your root.
Earth keep you covered
and nourish your small, shy shoot."

"Pip, pip," says yellow bird,
"Here is a wonder to see:
reaching for air and for sunlight,
a flourishing tree."

Worthless Will

For Guthrie, from Dad

Young Will Worthless, shepherd boy,
was paid to mind the sheep.
Instead he'd sprawl and suck a straw
and often fall asleep.

Counting Sheep

One for a ewe.
Two for a ram.
Three for a chop
or a leg of lamb.

Four for a baa.
Five for a bleat.
Six for the ticks
that nip your feet.

Oh for a life
that's rich and full,
instead of minding
balls of wool.

Counting sheep
is such a bore.
No wonder that
you start to snore.

One day, as Will lay fast asleep,
the sheep began to stray.
When, finally, he rubbed his eyes
the flock had slipped away.

Will got up and gave a shrug.
"They won't get very far.
They'll do no harm around the farm,
apart from bleat and baa."

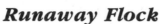

Runaway Flock

Dear, oh dear,
oh, what a disgrace!
Those sheep have strayed
all over the place.

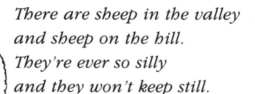

There are sheep in the valley
and sheep on the hill.
They're ever so silly
and they won't keep still.

There are sheep in the orchard
and sheep in the meadow,
and yikes! – there are sheep
in the farmer's bed, oh

how will we catch them
and what'll we do?
There are several sheep
in the farmhouse loo!

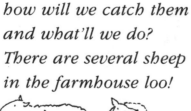

The barn is pulsing,
the farmyard's full
of bleating and baaing
and mutton and wool.

Get out of the way
or you're in for a shock.
For this is the day
of the runaway flock.

The farmer came and yelled with rage,
"You're paid to mind my sheep.
And yet they wander everywhere
while you lie fast asleep.

"Be off with you, you idle lad.
I'm giving you the sack."
So Will picked up his hat and stick
and went off down the track.

Journey

When it's time to set off
and the sky is blue,

where do you go
and what do you do?

How do you tell
which path to tread?

Follow your heart,
or follow your head?

Or follow a whisper
in the air

which leads you to...
I wonder where?

Will walked down the weary track
for half a day or more.
He stopped beneath a shady tree
because his feet were sore.

And there, among the roots, he spied
a tiny girl in red.
"Please help me out. I'm stuck," she cried.
"Why, certainly," Will said.

Fairy

A fairy may seem tiny,
a fairy may seem weak.
And, when she's stuck and struggling,
she may shed tears and squeak.

But if you meet a fairy,
be helpful and polite,
especially if she's in a fix,
caught up in something tight.

For when you're on life's highway,
before the deep, dark wood,
a fairy favour at your side
is bound to bring some good.

The tiny girl snapped off a branch.
She held it up to Will.
Then from her belt she drew a knife
And carved with silent skill.

She whittled out a whistle.
Then into it she blew.
"Its power will work three times," she said.
"It is my gift to you."

Magic Whistle

Magic whistle, carved from wood,
will you truly bring me good?

Can you keep me safe from harm
with your faery woodwind charm?

When I meet the fearsome foe
shall I trust to stand and blow?

What can magic music do?
Dare I now believe in you?

Will took the whistle, thanked the girl
and travelled down the road.
He soon came to a gully where
a rapid river flowed.

But squatting on the only bridge
there lurked an ugly troll.
"I'll eat you for my tea," it said,
"unless you pay my toll."

Troll

I'm a troll, foldy roll,
and I'm standing on my bridge.
I'm a troll, foldy roll,
and there's nothing in my fridge.
And I'm getting very hungry
for a nice sam-widge.
So I'll slap you on a slice
and I'll bite – SQUELCH! SQUIDGE!

Or I'll roll you and I'll fold you
in a big foldy roll.
Then I'll lick you and I'll stick you
in my great cake-hole.

I'm a troll, foldy roll,
and I aren't half strong.
And I'm big and I'm hairy
and I don't half pong.
And I gobble up people
though it's nasty and it's wrong.
Now it's time to give a roll
on my noisy dinner GONG!

For Will to carry on his way
he had to cross that river.
And yet he couldn't pass the troll –
its sheer size made him shiver.

So Will blew on his whistle.
(He hadn't any cash.)
The big troll leaped right off the bridge
and hit the water – SPLASH!

Beyond the bridge, the wood began,
so dark, with spooky trees.
"There'll be adventure here," thought Will.
"I smell it on the breeze."

He gripped his magic whistle tight
and stepped into the wood.
But soon before him on the path
a sturdy brigand stood.

Brigand

Brigand with your cudgel,
your pistol and your knife,
your eyes that pierce, they blaze so fierce
I tremble for my life.

Brigand with your brawny arms
and legs like lumps of meat,
when sight of you comes into view
my poor heart skips a beat.

Brigand with your bristly beard
and gruesome grisly grin,
I fear to pick a fight with you.
I worry that you'd win.

"Aha!" the beastly brigand growled.
"A traveller, and alone!
Hand over all you have, or else
I'll hack you flesh from bone!"

So Will blew on his whistle.
The brigand heard the sound.
At once he took his weapons off
and dropped them to the ground.

"I'll never steal again," he sighed.
"From now on I'll be good."
And, whistling as he went, he skipped off
gaily through the wood.

As young Will left the wood, he saw
a strange, enchanted town.
And on the hill a giant sat,
who gave a grumpy frown.

"Who dares to come this way?" he roared.
"This town belongs to me!
It feeds me people every day
for breakfast, lunch and tea."

Giant

Great, big giant
like a great, fat lump.

Great, big boots
go *thump, thump, thump*.

Great, big bottom
as heavy as a hill.

Great, big belly
so difficult to fill.

Tiny, little brain
in a great, big head.

Great, big giant,
we wish you were dead!

Will blew on his whistle.
It played a dancing tune.
The giant's toes began to tap
and he was dancing soon.

He danced so hard upon the hill
the earth began to crack.
It opened up and swallowed him
and never belched him back

Dance

Pick up a whistle,
play me an air.
Make me dance
from here to there.

Tap me a rhythm,
blow me a tune.
Blow me down,
I'm dancing soon!

Bliss in the body
and funk in the feet.
Music's power
has got me beat.

The people of the town ran out.
They all began to sing.
"You've saved us from that brute," they
    cheered.
"So come and be our king."

"That seems a good idea," thought Will.
"A king has wealth and fame.
I've landed on my feet here
and made myself a name.

"So, let's start with a party.
Fetch music, food and wine.
For this beats minding baa lambs.
A kingdom – and it's mine!"

Party

It's party time, it's party time.
We're dancing in the streets.

There's bubbly wine and clothes so fine
and showers of fancy sweets.

There's hot spaghetti and bright confetti
and music and games, and yes!

By the end of the night, we'll all look a fright
and there'll be one hell of a mess.

But Will was not the kind of lad
to make a careful king.
He liked to laze about and dream
or else to dance and sing.

He picked his empty whistle up
to while the time away.
And very soon, yes, tune by tune,
he'd taught himself to play.

He should've sat upon his throne
to see fair justice done.
Instead he played his whistle
and filled the air with fun.

Frolic

Skip to the tune that drips from my whistle,
skip, skip, skip.
And the butlers drop their bottles
as their toes all start to trip.

Dance to the air that whirls from my whistle,
dance, dance, dance.
And the maids all let their dusters drift
as they start to swirl and prance.

Jig to the notes that spring from my whistle,
jig, jig, jig.
And the clerk soon screws his scroll up
and the chamberlain chucks his wig.

Rave to the racket that wails from my whistle,
rave, rave, rave.
And the Court's caught up in chaos
and forgets how it ought to behave!

The Council came to caution Will
to keep himself in check.
"The Court's become," they sternly said,
"A crazy discotheque!"

Just then a band of players passed by.
They looked so light and free.
"Ah, that's more like it," sighed young Will.
"Now, that's the life for me."

Players

One to dance with leaps and kicks.
One to show strange magic tricks.
One to walk a trembling wire.
One to juggle brands of fire.
One to sing a stirring song.
One to beat on drum and gong.
One to fool about and clown...
And one to pipe them through the town!

He left his robe of kingship.
He left his golden crown.
He left his royal signet ring
and put his sceptre down.

He left his cosy castle,
his clean and comfy bed.
He changed his fancy costume
for his simple clothes instead.

And off went worthless Will once more,
to join the jolly band,
to pipe at parties, feasts and fairs
across the lively land.

Away

Over the hills and far away
together we shall pipe and play,
and woo the world with clever tricks
and stunning feats and juggling sticks.

On through valley, over plain,
round the world and back again,
travelling on through any weather,
in one merry band together.

And who's that walking just ahead?
Why, yes! The tiny girl in red!

153

Praise for Tony Mitton's poetry:

The Red and White
Spotted Handkerchief

"This is a book to treasure."

School Library Association

"The verse is simple and accessible and the line
drawings irresistible."

Daily Mail

"A sparkling collection of poems that tell of three
magical adventures, with illustrations to stimulate
minds young and old. One to treasure."

Right Start

"Narrative poems have charms for listeners of all ages. Tony Mitton exploits this traditional form skilfully in *The Red and White Spotted Handkerchief*."

Glasgow Herald

"Tony Mitton's second collection of children's verse, *The Red and White Spotted Handkerchief*, more than lives up to the promise of his first book, *Plum*. If you buy only one volume of children's poetry this year, let it be this handsomely jacketed and illustrated narrative sequence."

Michael Thorn, Literary Review

Plum

"*Plum* is a first collection by Tony Mitton and
it's a treat ... here is a book by a man who likes writing
poetry and wants his readers to enjoy it, too."

Lindsey Fraser, Guardian

"The children loved the way the poems posed
so many questions, but never gave any answers.
This was the anthology that everyone wanted to own."

Carousel

"Bailey's pen-and-ink drawings effortlessly amplify the
many moods, voices and landscapes of Tony Mitton's verse
– from the humorous, the playful and the whimsical, to the
mystical, the metaphysical, the pagan and the folklorish."

Literacy and Learning

"*Plum* is so good a debut collection that Tony Mitton
might just be the next Charles Causley of children's
poetry."

Times Educational Supplement